Blastoff! Readers are carefully developed by literacy experts to build reading stamina and move students toward fluency by combining standards-based content with developmentally appropriate text.

Level 1 provides the most support through repetition of high-frequency words, light text, predictable sentence patterns, and strong visual support.

Level 2 offers early readers a bit more challenge through varied sentences, increased text load, and text-supportive special features.

Level 3 advances early-fluent readers toward fluency through increased text load, less reliance on photos, advancing concepts, longer sentences, and more complex special features.

★ **Blastoff! Universe**

Reading Level

Grade K

Grades 1–3

Grade 4

This edition first published in 2023 by Bellwether Media, Inc.

No part of this publication may be reproduced in whole or in part without written permission of the publisher. For information regarding permission, write to Bellwether Media, Inc., Attention: Permissions Department, 6012 Blue Circle Drive, Minnetonka, MN 55343.

Library of Congress Cataloging-in-Publication Data

Names: Barnes, Rachael, author.
Title: Germany / by Rachael Barnes.
Description: Minneapolis, MN : Bellwether Media, Inc., 2023. | Series: Blastoff! Readers : countries of the world | Includes bibliographical references and index. | Audience: Ages 5-8 | Audience: Grades 2-3 | Summary: "Relevant images match informative text in this introduction to Germany. Intended for students in kindergarten through third grade"– Provided by publisher.
Identifiers: LCCN 2022044145 (print) | LCCN 2022044146 (ebook) | ISBN 9798886871302 (library binding) | ISBN 9798886872569 (ebook)
Subjects: LCSH: Germany–Juvenile literature.
Classification: LCC DD17 .B33 2023 (print) | LCC DD17 (ebook) | DDC 943–dc23/eng/20220915
LC record available at https://lccn.loc.gov/2022044145
LC ebook record available at https://lccn.loc.gov/2022044146

Text copyright © 2023 by Bellwether Media, Inc. BLASTOFF! READERS and associated logos are trademarks and/or registered trademarks of Bellwether Media, Inc.

Editor: Elizabeth Neuenfeldt   Designer: Gabriel Hilger

Printed in the United States of America, North Mankato, MN.

Table of Contents

All About Germany	4
Land and Animals	6
Life in Germany	12
Germany Facts	20
Glossary	22
To Learn More	23
Index	24

All About Germany

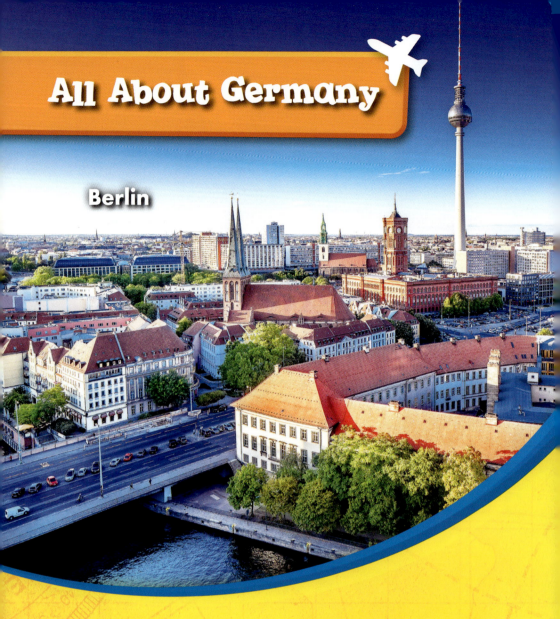

Berlin

Germany is a country in Europe. Berlin is the capital city.

Famous **composers** have called Germany home. The country is known for its castles, too!

Land and Animals

Plains cover northern Germany. Hills and mountains rise farther south. Small lakes dot the country.

The Rhine River runs along western Germany. The Black Forest fills the southwest.

Rhine River

Black Forest

Size: 2,320 square miles (6,009 square kilometers)

Famous For: large forest that is the setting of many German fairy tales

Germany has **temperate** weather. Summers are mild. Winters are cool and wet.

More rain falls near the North Sea. Southern mountains receive the most snow.

North Sea

Eurasian badgers build **burrows** in the Black Forest. Red deer munch on trees.

Eurasian badger

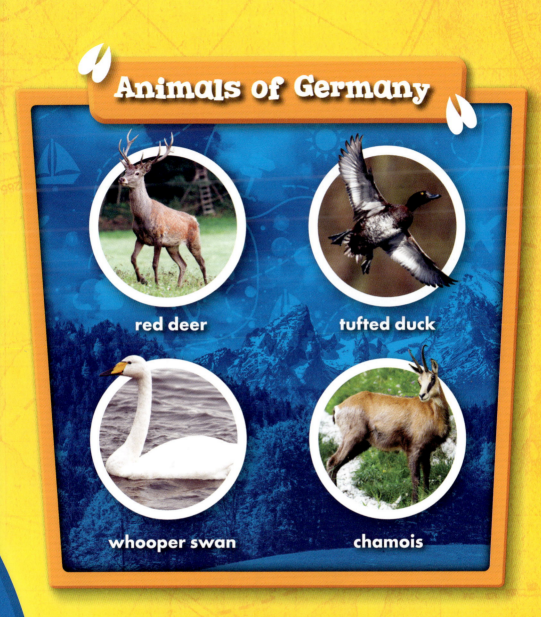

Tufted ducks and whooper swans fly over rivers and lakes. Chamois run on the mountains.

Life in Germany

Most Germans live in cities. Families often live in apartments.

German is the national language. Many people have German **ancestors**. Many Germans are **Christians**.

apartments

Soccer is a popular sport in Germany. People also like to swim and hike.

14

Germans enjoy music. They attend concerts and **festivals**. At home, families play board games.

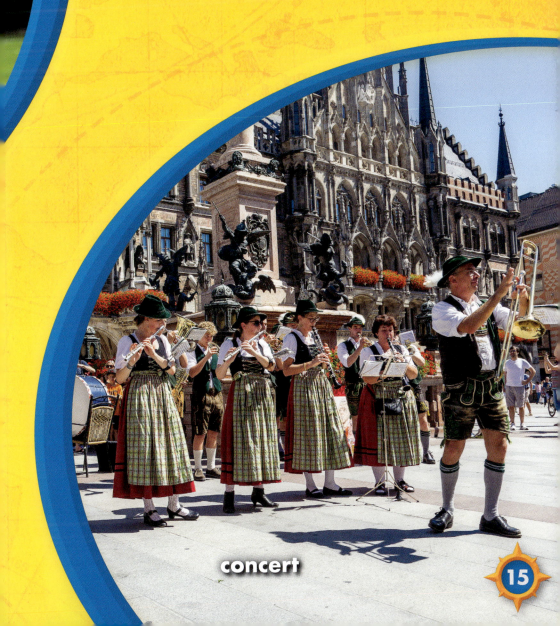

concert

Potatoes are a German **staple**. They are used in potato dumplings. Bratwurst and sauerkraut are also popular.

German Foods

potato dumplings

bratwurst and sauerkraut

rye bread

gingersnaps

making rye bread

Rye bread is often eaten with jam. Gingersnaps are a tasty treat!

Oktoberfest

Oktoberfest is a popular fall festival. Visitors enjoy food and rides!

Christmas is in December. Families visit Christmas markets. They give gifts and decorate trees. Many people enjoy German **traditions**!

Germany Facts

Size:
137,847 square miles (357,022 square kilometers)

Population:
84,316,622 (2022)

National Holiday:
Unity Day (October 3)

Main Language:
German

Capital City:
Berlin

Famous Face

Name: Thomas Müller

Famous For: soccer player with one World Cup and many championship wins

Religions

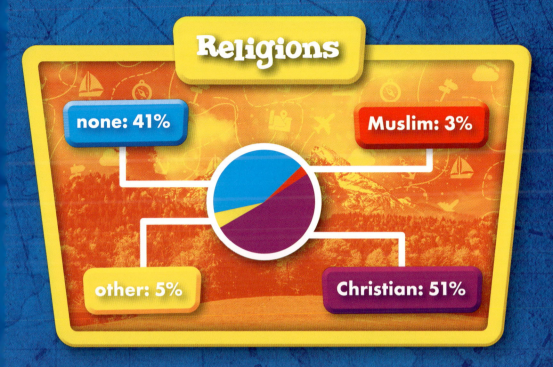

- none: 41%
- Muslim: 3%
- other: 5%
- Christian: 51%

Top Landmarks

Berchtesgaden National Park

Miniatur Wunderland

Neuschwanstein Castle

21

Glossary

ancestors—relatives who lived long ago

burrows—holes or tunnels some animals dig for homes

Christians—people who believe in the words of Jesus Christ

composers—people who write music

festivals—times or events of celebration

plains—large areas of flat land

staple—a widely used food or other item

temperate—related to weather that is not too hot or too cold

traditions—customs, ideas, or beliefs handed down from one generation to the next

To Learn More

AT THE LIBRARY
Blevins, Wiley. *Germany*. New York N.Y.: Scholastic, 2018.

Boone, Mary. *Let's Look at Germany*. North Mankato, Minn.: Capstone, 2020.

Thuras, Dylan. *The Atlas Obscura Explorer's Guide for the World's Most Adventurous Kid*. New York, N.Y.: Workman Publishing, 2018.

ON THE WEB

FACTSURFER

Factsurfer.com gives you a safe, fun way to find more information.

1. Go to www.factsurfer.com.
2. Enter "Germany" into the search box and click 🔍.
3. Select your book cover to see a list of related content.

Index

animals, 10, 11
Berlin, 4, 5
Black Forest, 6, 7, 10
board games, 15
capital (see Berlin)
castles, 5
Christmas, 19
cities, 12
composers, 5
Europe, 4
food, 16, 17
German, 12, 13
Germany facts, 20–21
hike, 14
lakes, 6, 11
map, 5
mountains, 6, 9, 11
music, 15
North Sea, 9

Oktoberfest, 18
people, 12, 14
plains, 6
Rhine River, 6
say hello, 13
soccer, 14
summers, 8
swim, 14
weather, 8
winters, 8

The images in this book are reproduced through the courtesy of: canadastock, cover; Wolfilser, cover; Rolf G Wackenberg, p. 3; frank_peters, pp. 4-5; Freeartist, p. 6; Funny Solution Studio, pp. 6-7; 13threephotography, pp. 8-9; Harald Lueder, p. 9; Vaclav Matous, pp. 10-11; Frantisek Hromada, p. 11 (red deer); Maciej Olszewski, p. 11 (tufted duck); jack perks, p. 11 (whooper swan); Porojnicu Stelian, p. 11 (chamois); ali caliskan, p. 12; Osana Trautwein, pp. 12-13; DieterMeyrl, p. 14 (inset); Michele Morrone, pp. 14-15; Sergii Figurnyi, p. 15; Karl Allgaeuer, p. 16 (potato dumplings); George Dolgikh, p. 16 (bratwurst and sauerkraut); Dar1930, p. 16 (rye bread); Brent Hofacker, p. 16 (gingersnaps); dpa picture alliance/ Alamy, p. 17; FooTToo, pp. 18-19; titoOnz, p. 20 (flag); Martin Rose/ Staff/ Getty Images, p. 20 (Thomas Müller); Rasto SK, p. 21 (Berchtesgaden National Park); Ritu Manoj Jethani, p. 21 (Miniatur Wunderland); Vadym Larva, p. 21 (Neuschwanstein Castle); MMCez, pp. 22-23.

24